CAKE POPS

KIT *by Bakerella*

Step-by-Step Instructions for Making
the Cutest Cake Pops Ever!

BY ANGIE DUDLEY

CHRONICLE BOOKS
SAN FRANCISCO

Library of Congress Cataloging-in-Publication
Data available.

ISBN 978-1-4521-0292-4

Manufactured in China

Designed by Emily Dubin

10 9 8 7 6 5 4 3 2 1

Chronicle Books LLC
680 Second Street
San Francisco, California 94107
www.chroniclebooks.com

Contents

Introduction

Cake pops, cupcake pops, cake balls, and bites. They all have the same things in common: cake, frosting, candy, and cute. But these aren't ordinary cakes. They are tiny candy-covered confections made of crumbled cake mixed with frosting that you can mold into different shapes and decorate for any occasion.

I had so much fun creating the *Cake Pops* book; I wanted to follow it up with something really exciting. So, welcome to the *Cake Pops Kit*! With some of my favorite cake pops, like Spring Chicks and Panda Bears, and some new ones, like Penguins and Rubber Duckies, this cute little kit gives you easy-to-follow, step-by-step instructions for making ten different cake pops—plus everything you need to wrap up and give these treats to your family and friends.

You'll find plenty of cake pop–sized treat bags, lollipop sticks, color-ful ribbon, and gorgeously designed gift tags. There's even a Cake Pop Stand, the perfect spot to put your pops while you're working on them and pretty enough to present your finished pops too.

Five of the projects are from the original book, and I've added five more, including pretty little Penguins, Buzzing Bumblebees, Wedding Cake Pops, Rubber Duckies, and sweet Burger Bites (no stick necessary!). Need something unique for your next party? The answer is right here. But be careful: Once you make them, you won't want to stop. And anyone that eats one probably won't let you.

If you are just starting out in the world of cake pops, the basics are in here, too, from the simple cake ball to the cake pop to the now-famous cupcake pops.

And don't worry. You don't have to be a pastry artist or confection-ery genius to make cake pops. (I'm not a professional baker, and I don't have any formal training, so you don't have to either.) You don't even need to be a great baker. With a few ingredients and common candy, you can transform any cake, even a store-bought one, into fascinating tiny treats.

You'll learn the methods behind the madness. You'll see how easy they are to decorate. You'll learn techniques that will kick-start your creativity. Once you make your first cake pop, you'll be so proud of what you've accomplished. I promise.

Let's get started!

Planning Ahead

Being organized will save you a lot of time and unnecessary frustration. You don't want to be counting out candies for decorating when you're dipping cake pops. Make sure everything is within easy reach. Sprinkles can go in small dishes, and lollipop sticks can stand in a small glass. You can also make the cake the night before and let it cool. Then your time the next day can be devoted to dipping and decorating.

Are four dozen cake pops too many? You can make as few as a dozen at a time. Each quarter section of cake yields about 12 cake pops (and the included Cake Pop Stand holds 12, too). Remember to adjust the amount of frosting accordingly. Just freeze the extra cake quarter sections and save for later use.

Keep in mind that dark-colored cakes may show through white or light-colored coatings. If you want the coating to be completely opaque, try dipping a second time.

Light-colored frostings work better with light-colored cakes. The frosting blends right in and disappears.

CANDY COATING BASICS

Candy coating, also referred to as candy wafers, compound coatings, confectionery coating, chocolate bark, bark coating, and candy melts, is used in candy making. It can be used for dipping, in candy molds, or even in squeeze bottles for piping or drizzling. Candy coating comes in a variety of colors and flavors. It is easy to use and doesn't require tempering, as chocolate does. Just melt and use.

Store coatings in a cool, dry place until ready to use. Do not store in the refrigerator or freezer. If stored properly, leftover candy coatings can even be reheated and used again.

It doesn't hurt to keep an extra bag of candy coating on hand for the color you are using just in case. You can always use it for a future project if you don't need it.

MELTING METHODS To use candy coating, simply melt the amount you need and you're ready to go. Rather than melting all of the candy coating at once, I usually work with about 1 lb/455 g at a time. Try one of the following methods to find the one that appeals to you most.

Microwave: Melt candy coating in a microwave-safe bowl. Microwave on medium power in 30-second intervals, stirring in between. Repeat until the coating is completely melted. When you first stir, the coating will still be firm. That's okay; just keep repeating, making sure not to overheat the coating. In addition, be sure not to let any water mix with the coating.

Double boiler: I don't usually use this method because most of the time I melt more than one color of candy coating, and it's easier to use the microwave and work with smaller bowls. However, if you are using one color, the double boiler method is a great alternative. Fill the bottom section of a double boiler with water and bring to a simmer. Remove it from the heat and place candy coating in the top section. Stir continuously until completely melted and smooth.

Warming tray: A warming tray allows you to use several oven-safe bowls at one time. Make sure they are small and deep enough for dipping. Turn the tray on low and you will be able to keep multiple colors melted.

THINNING CANDY COATING Working with candy coating can be lots of fun, but only if it is working with you. Sometimes the coating is too thick, making it more difficult to dip the cake pops. Darker-colored coatings sometimes have this problem. An easy way to thin the coating is to use a product called

paramount crystals (pictured above), adding a few pieces to the coating. Stir until melted and fluid. You can also use regular shortening or even vegetable oil as an alternative. Start by adding just 1 tsp. Stir in until melted. Add more as needed until the coating is fluid enough to work with easily.

USING CHOCOLATE AS A COATING SUBSTITUTE
Regular chocolate can be used as a substitute for candy coating, but keep in mind that the coatings are made to do just that—coat. Baking chocolate and morsels will cover the cake balls, but will not harden in the same way that candy coating will. Therefore, this alternative is best when making cake balls instead of cake pops, because the pops need a hard coating to give them extra stability on the sticks.

You may also need to thin chocolate with shortening or paramount crystals to make it more fluid.

COLORING CANDY COATING
Although candy coating comes in a variety of colors, sometimes you need to tint your own to get just the right shade. Tinting white candy coating is also a great alternative if you need only a small amount of one color and don't want to buy a whole package of coating. Add a few drops of candy coloring to start. Add more color, a few drops at a time, until you achieve the shade you desire. If you add too much color, you can lighten it by adding more white candy coating.

Make sure to use oil-based candy coloring and not regular food coloring, which contains water. Food coloring will ruin the coating.

ADDING FLAVORINGS
Besides adding color to your candy coating, you can also flavor it with candy oils. These intense flavorings are stronger than the regular flavorings and extracts you'll find in the baking section of the grocery store. You need to use only a small amount. Some flavor examples are blueberry, bubblegum, watermelon, and peppermint.

THE DIPPING METHOD

The question I have been asked the most is, "How do you get your coating so smooth?" Well, it's really simple.

Use small bowls of melted candy coating about 3 in/7.5 cm deep. Make sure the coating is thin enough to dip and remove easily. You can use paramount crystals, shortening, or even vegetable oil to thin coatings. And then just tap excess coating off gently using the following method.

Make sure your coating is deep enough to allow you to completely submerge the firmed cake pop. Small, narrow, and deep microwave-safe plastic bowls are best, so you can hold the bowl easily without burning any fingers. Glass bowls can get too hot. Dip about ½ in/12 mm of a lollipop stick into the melted coating and insert it into a cake ball, pushing it no more than halfway through.

Then dip the cake pop in the melted coating, completely covering the cake ball, and remove it in one motion. If the coating is too thick, gently tap off any excess. Hold it over the bowl in your left hand, and tap your left wrist gently with your right hand. If you use the hand holding the cake pop to shake off excess coating, the force of

the movement will be too strong and could cause the cake ball to loosen or fly off the lollipop stick. Tapping the wrist holding the cake pop absorbs some of the impact. The excess coating will fall off, but you will need to rotate the lollipop stick so the coating doesn't build up on one side, making it too heavy on that side. If too much coating starts to build up at the base of the stick, simply use your finger to wipe it off, spinning the lollipop stick at the same time. This can happen if the coating is too thin or too hot. It's not hard; it just takes practice.

USING CANDY COATING AS "GLUE" After your cake pops are coated and dry, you can use any remaining candy coating left in your dipping bowl as glue. Apply it to candy or sprinkles with a toothpick and attach them to the cake pop. You can also apply it to a coated, dry cake ball and then place the add-on into position. Use a tiny amount of coating to attach the smallest items, such as sprinkles. Use a slightly larger amount for bigger add-ons, such as M&M's or candy necklace pieces. When the coating dries, the add-on will be attached, or "glued" on. If the coating in the bowl has dried, simply heat it again to melt it.

Dipping Do's & Don'ts

- Do use a bowl deep enough to dip your cake pops and remove them in one motion.

- Don't get any water in your candy coating.

- Do keep a dry dish towel or paper towels nearby to wipe off your hands.

- Don't overheat your candy coating.

- Do use shortening or paramount crystals to thin coating that is too thick.

- Don't use regular food coloring to tint candy coating.

- Do use special candy coloring to tint it.

- Don't dip frozen cake balls. Firm, yes. Frozen, no.

- Do dip the sticks in melted coating before you insert them into cake pops.

- Don't push lollipop sticks more than halfway through the cake ball.

- Do have a lot of fun.

MY TWO FAVORITE TOOLS

EDIBLE-INK PENS Dot your eyes. Edible-ink pens are an excellent tool to have on hand if you decide to add personality to your cake pops. They are quick and easy. Use them to draw eyes, mouths, eyelashes, and more. Americolor Gourmet Writer pens come in colors like black, brown, pink, red, blue, and more. You can buy a whole set or just black to suit your need.

Use them carefully. If you press down too hard when drawing on the candy coating, residue from the candy will build up on the tip, making the pens difficult to use. So use a very light touch. Imagine the pen as a paintbrush and the pops as your canvas. When dotting eyes on sprinkles, though, you'll need to press a little harder.

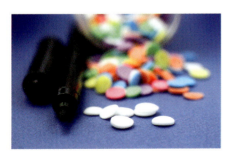

TOOTHPICKS Always keep a small container of toothpicks within reach.

You can use them to direct candy coating that may not have made its way completely around a cake pop. You can use it to texturize the surface of the candy coating. Or, if your candy coating pools at the bottom of cake balls after they are placed on a wax paper–covered baking sheet to dry, simply take a toothpick and draw a line through the coating, close to the cake ball. When it dries, you can break off the unwanted coating for a cleaner look.

Toothpicks are also extremely useful when adding decorations. Dip the end of a toothpick into melted candy coating and dot a little bit in position for small add-ons like sprinkles for eyes.

The Basics

Over the next few pages, you'll find easy instructions that will help you master three of the methods of creating unique sweet treats— Basic Cake Balls, Basic Cake Pops, and Basic Cupcake Pops. Get ready to impress your friends, your family, and even yourself.

The following how-to's are based on using a cake mix and ready-made frosting. It's a really easy way to learn the basics and achieve predictable, consistent results. Then, once you feel comfortable making and decorating your very own cake pops, you'll have the knowledge to branch out with other cake and frosting recipes and get even more creative with custom flavors.

Or just stick with the mixes. I do.

Basic Cake Balls

Cake balls are super-easy to make and form the basis of endless variations of decorated cake pops and cupcake pops.

MAKES 48 CAKE BALLS

1. Bake the cake as directed on the box, using a 9-by-13-in/ 23-by-33-cm cake pan. Let cool completely.

2. Once the cake has cooled, get organized and set aside plenty of time (at least an hour) to crumble, roll, and dip four dozen cake balls.

3. Crumble the cooled cake into a large mixing bowl. You should not see any large pieces of cake.

4. Add three-quarters of the container of frosting. (You will not need the remaining frosting.) Mix it into the crumbled cake, using the back of a large metal spoon, until thoroughly combined. If you use the entire container, the cake balls will be too moist.

5. The mixture should be moist enough to roll into 1½-in/ 4-cm balls and still hold a round shape. After rolling the cake balls by hand, place them on a wax paper–covered baking sheet.

6. Cover with plastic wrap and chill for several hours in the refrigerator, or place in the freezer for about 15 minutes. You want the balls to be firm but not frozen.

(If you're making a project that calls for uncoated cake balls, stop here and proceed to decorate the cake balls, following the project instructions.)

continued

YOU'LL NEED

18.25-oz/520-g box cake mix

9-by-13-in/23-by-33-cm cake pan

Large mixing bowl

16-oz/455-g container ready-made frosting

Large metal spoon

Wax paper

Two baking sheets

Plastic wrap

2 lb/910 g candy coating

Deep, microwave-safe plastic bowl

Toothpicks

Squeeze bottle or resealable plastic bag (optional)

7. Place the candy coating in a deep, microwave-safe plastic bowl. These bowls make it easier to cover the cake balls completely with candy coating while holding the bowl without burning your fingers. (I usually work with about 1 lb/455 g of coating at a time.)

8. Melt the candy coating, following the instructions on the package. Microwave on medium power for 30 seconds at a time, stirring with a spoon in between. You can also use a double boiler. Either way, make sure you do not overheat the coating. See "Candy Coating Basics," page 8, for more on working with candy coating.

9. Now you're ready to coat. Take a few cake balls out of the refrigerator or freezer to work with at a time. If they're in the freezer, transfer the rest of the balls to the refrigerator at this point, so they stay firm but do not freeze.

10. Place one ball at a time into the melted candy coating. Spoon extra coating over any uncoated areas of the cake ball to make sure it is completely covered in candy coating. Then lift out the cake ball with your spoon. Avoid stirring it in the coating, because cake crumbs can fall off into the coating.

continued

11. Holding the spoon over the bowl, tap the handle of the spoon several times on the edge of the bowl until the excess coating falls off and back into the bowl. This technique also creates a smooth surface on the outside of the cake ball.

12. Transfer the coated cake ball to another wax paper–covered baking sheet to dry. Let the coated cake ball slide right off the spoon. Some coating may pool around the base of the ball onto the wax paper. If so, simply take a toothpick and use it to draw a line around the base of the cake ball before the coating sets. Once the coating sets, you can break off any unwanted coating.

13. Repeat with the remaining cake balls and let dry completely.

14. If you have extra candy coating left over, pour it into a squeeze bottle (or a resealable plastic bag and then snip off a corner) and drizzle it over the tops in a zigzag motion to decorate.

15. Store them in an airtight container on the counter or in the refrigerator for several days. If you are giving them away as gifts, you can cover and tie them with the treat bags and ribbon and add gift tags.

Tip

- *Creating Shapes* Crumbled cake mixed with frosting can easily be rolled by hand into round balls. It can also be molded into oval, rectangular, or triangular shapes. Subtle changes in shape can change a penguin into an owl.

Basic Cake Pops

Once you know how to make a basic cake pop, it's easy to start making the projects in the kit or create your own designs.

MAKES 48 CAKE POPS

1. Bake the cake as directed on the box, using a 9-by-13-in/ 23-by-33-cm cake pan. Let cool completely.

2. Once the cake has cooled, get organized and set aside plenty of time (a couple of hours) to crumble, roll, and dip four dozen cake pops.

3. Crumble the cooled cake into a large mixing bowl. You should not see any large pieces of cake.

4. Add three-quarters of the container of frosting. (You will not need the remaining frosting.) Mix it into the crumbled cake, using the back of a large metal spoon, until thoroughly combined. If you use the entire container, the cake balls will be too moist.

5. The mixture should be moist enough to roll into 1½-in/ 4-cm balls and still hold a round shape. After rolling the cake balls by hand, place them on wax paper–covered baking sheets.

6. Cover with plastic wrap and chill for several hours in the refrigerator, or place in the freezer for about 15 minutes. You want the balls to be firm but not frozen.

7. Place the candy coating in a deep, microwave-safe plastic bowl. These bowls make it easier to cover the cake balls completely with candy coating while holding the bowl without burning your fingers. (I usually work with about 1 lb/455 g of coating at a time.)

continued

YOU'LL NEED

18.25-oz/520-g box cake mix

9-by-13-in/23-by-33-cm cake pan

Large mixing bowl

16-oz/455-g container ready-made frosting

Large metal spoon

Wax paper

Two baking sheets

Plastic wrap

3 lb/1.4 kg candy coating

Deep, microwave-safe plastic bowl

48 paper lollipop sticks

Cake Pops Stand or a Styrofoam block

8. Melt the candy coating, following the instructions on the package. Microwave on medium power for 30 seconds at a time, stirring with a spoon in between. You can also use a double boiler. Either way, make sure you do not overheat the coating. See "Candy Coating Basics," page 8, for more on working with candy coating.

9. Now you're ready to dip. Take a few cake balls out of the refrigerator or freezer to work with. If they're in the freezer, transfer the rest of the balls to the refrigerator at this point, so they stay firm but do not freeze.

10. One at a time, dip about $1/2$ in/12 mm of the tip of a lollipop stick into the melted candy coating, and insert the stick straight into a cake ball, pushing it no more than halfway through.

11. Holding the lollipop stick with cake ball attached, dip the entire cake ball into the melted candy coating until it is completely covered, and remove it in one motion. Make sure the coating meets at the base of the lollipop stick. This helps secure the cake ball to the stick when the coating sets. The object is to completely cover the cake ball and remove it without submerging it in the coating more than once. If you do resubmerge the cake pop, the weight of the candy coating can pull on the cake ball and cause it to get stuck in the coating.

continued

(The thinner the consistency of your coating, the easier it will be to coat the cake pops. If you find that your coating is too thick, add some shortening or paramount crystals to help thin it and make the coating more fluid.)

12. When you remove the cake pop from the candy coating, some excess coating may start to drip. Hold the cake pop in one hand and use the other hand to gently tap the first wrist. Rotate the lollipop stick if necessary to allow the excess coating to fall off evenly, so one side doesn't get heavier than the other. If you didn't completely dunk the cake pop, this method of tapping and rotating generally takes care of that. The coating will slowly slide down the surface of the cake ball until it reaches the lollipop stick.

If too much coating surrounds the base of the lollipop stick, you can wipe the excess off with your finger. Simply place your finger on the stick right under the cake ball and rotate the pop, allowing any excess coating to fall off and back into the bowl of coating. When most of the excess coating has fallen off and it is no longer dripping, stick the cake pop into the stand.

13. Repeat with the remaining cake balls and let dry completely.

14. Store them in an airtight container on the counter or in the refrigerator for several days. If you are giving them away as gifts, you can cover and tie them with the treat bags and ribbon and add gift tags.

Basic Cupcake Pops

With a small flower-shaped metal cookie cutter, you can easily turn a basic cake pop into a cute cupcake pop.

MAKES 48 CUPCAKE POPS

1. Bake the cake as directed on the box, using a 9-by-13-in/ 23-by-33-cm cake pan. Let cool completely.

2. Once the cake has cooled, get organized and set aside plenty of time (a couple of hours) to crumble, roll, shape, dip, and decorate four dozen cupcake pops. (If it feels more manageable, cut the cake in quarters, put three in the freezer and use one to make a dozen pops at a time.)

3. Crumble the cooled cake into a large mixing bowl. You should not see any large pieces of cake.

4. Add three-quarters of the container of frosting (don't forget to use less frosting if you are only making 12 pops; you will not need the remaining frosting). Mix it into the crumbled cake, using the back of a large metal spoon, until thoroughly combined. If you use the entire container, the cake balls will be too moist.

5. The mixture should be moist enough to roll into 1½-in/ 4-cm balls and still hold a round shape. After rolling the cake balls by hand, place them on a wax paper–covered baking sheet.

6. Cover with plastic wrap and chill for several hours in the refrigerator, or place in the freezer for about 15 minutes. You want the balls to be firm but not frozen.

   continued

YOU'LL NEED

18.25-oz/520-g box cake mix

9-by-13-in/23-by-33-cm cake pan

Large mixing bowl

16-oz/455-g container ready-made frosting

Large metal spoon

Wax paper

Two baking sheets

Plastic wrap

Flower-shaped cookie cutter (1¼ in/3 cm wide by ¾ in/ 2 cm deep)

2 lb/910 g chocolate candy coating

Two deep, microwave-safe plastic bowls

Dish towel

48 paper lollipop sticks

1 lb/455 g pink candy coating

Toothpicks

7. Remove the baking sheet from the refrigerator or freezer and begin shaping the cake balls into cupcakes. Take a chilled ball and roll it into a cylinder shape. Then slide it into the flower-shaped cookie cutter. The cake mixture should fill the entire cutter, with any excess forming a mounded cupcake top on one side. You can use your thumb to keep the shape flat on one side, allowing the rest to form a mound on the other. When you have the shape the way you like it, gently push the shaped cupcake out of the cutter from the bottom. If the mixture is still firm enough, you should also be able to gently pull it out by holding the top mounded side.

8. Place the cupcake-shaped cake ball, right-side up, back on the wax paper–covered baking sheet.

9. Continue with the remaining cake balls.

10. Once the balls are all shaped into cupcakes, return them to the freezer for 5 to 10 minutes to keep them firm.

11. Place the chocolate candy coating in a deep, microwave-safe plastic bowl. These bowls make it easier to dip the cupcake bottoms completely in candy coating while holding the bowl without burning your fingers. (I usually work with about 1 lb/455 g of coating at a time.)

12. Melt the candy coating, following the instructions on the package. Microwave on medium power for 30 seconds at a time, stirring with a spoon in between. You can also

continued

M&M's or similarly shaped candies

Sprinkles

Cake Pop Stand or Styrofoam block

use a double boiler. Either way, make sure you do not overheat the coating. See "Candy Coating Basics," page 8, for more on working with candy coating.

13. Now you're ready to dip. Take a few cupcake-shaped cake balls out of the freezer to work with. Transfer the rest to the refrigerator at this point, so they stay firm but do not freeze.

14. One at a time, take a cupcake-shaped cake ball and, holding it by the mounded top, dip the bottom into the melted chocolate candy coating—just to the point where the mounded shape starts. Remove it from the chocolate, turn it upside down, and swirl your hand in a circular motion. This will cause any excess chocolate coating to slide down. When the coating reaches the bottom of the mounded cupcake top shape, you can stop. Have a dish towel handy to wipe off your fingertips, as it is highly likely that you'll get some coating on them. Don't use water to rinse your hands, as getting water in the coating can make it unusable.

15. Place the half-coated cupcake shape on a second wax paper–covered baking sheet, chocolate candy coating–side up, mounded-side down. Immediately dip about $1/2$ in/12 mm of the tip of a lollipop stick into the melted candy coating, and insert the stick straight into the flat, chocolate-coated bottom of the cupcake while the chocolate is still wet. Push it no more than halfway through.

continued

16. Continue with the rest of the cupcake-shaped cake balls.

17. Allow the chocolate to dry completely.

18. Melt the pink candy coating in the same way that you melted the chocolate. You will now decorate the tops. This all comes together quickly, resulting in a finished cupcake pop.

19. Holding its lollipop stick, dip the top of a cupcake in the melted pink candy coating. It should completely cover the rest of the exposed cupcake and meet the edge of the chocolate coating.

20. Remove the cupcake pop from the coating and turn it right-side up. If the coating is too hot, it will start to drip down the sides. If this happens, let the coating sit for a few minutes to cool and start to thicken. Then when you dip the tops, the coating will stay in place.

21. While the coating is still wet, use a toothpick to touch up any areas the coating may not have covered. Then place an M&M (M-side down) on the top and add sprinkles for decoration.

22. Place the cupcake pop in the stand to dry completely. Repeat with the remaining cupcake pops.

23. Store them in an airtight container on the counter or in the refrigerator for several days. If you are giving them away as gifts, you can cover and tie them with the treat bags and ribbon and add gift tags.

Tip

- You can make these without lollipop sticks. They're just as cute.

TROUBLESHOOTING

You followed the directions but still need a little more help. Take a look at some of the following scenarios to see if you can find the answer.

YOUR CAKE IS TOO MOIST AND WILL NOT HOLD ITS SHAPE WHEN ROLLED INTO A BALL. You probably used too much frosting in proportion to cake. Add more cake to balance it out. Try crumbling in a few store-bought cupcakes, minus the frosting.

YOUR COATING WON'T COVER THE CAKE BALL SMOOTHLY. Make sure the balls are firm and not frozen. Frozen cake balls mixed with hot candy coating will cause the coating to start to set too quickly, often before the cake ball can be coated properly. If your cake balls are chilled properly and the coating still won't cover them smoothly, make sure you are using the appropriate dipping technique (see page 11).

YOU CAN'T FIND CANDY COATING. Try melting regular chocolate, and use shortening or paramount crystals to make it easier for dipping. This alternative is best used when making cake balls, because chocolate does not set as hard as candy coating does, making it less suitable for supporting cake pops on their sticks.

YOU MADE CAKE POPS AND THE COATING CRACKED. You may have rolled the cake balls too tightly. And if placed in the freezer for too long, the cake may have tried to expand, resulting in a crack in the coating. Don't worry; they won't fall off the stick if they've been secured by coating at the base. And you can even dip them a second time to fix it up or drizzle or decorate in a way to disguise the crack. I've seen this happen with cake pops, but not with cupcake pops or bites, because these methods use a two-part dipping method and give the cake ball or cupcake shape time to breathe before being completely coated.

YOUR CANDY COATING IS TOO THICK. Don't turn up the heat. Making the candy coating hotter doesn't make it thinner. If your coating is melted and is still too thick, add shortening or paramount crystals to the melted coating until it is thin enough to work with.

YOUR CAKE POPS KEEP FALLING OFF THE STICKS. Make sure the shaped cake balls are firm but not frozen when you dip them. If they start to get too soft, just return them to the freezer for a few minutes to firm them up again. Make sure the coating is thin enough to dip and remove in one motion. Don't stir the cake pops in the coating. Also make sure that you don't insert sticks more than halfway through the cake pops. Finally, check that the coating surrounds the cake ball at the base where the lollipop stick is inserted. Use a toothpick if necessary to direct the coating around the base of the stick.

CAKE OR OIL IS TRYING TO PUSH ITS WAY OUT OF THE POP. Make sure the pop is completely coated. Even the tiniest opening will invite the cake to try and escape.

CAKE CRUMBS ARE GETTING MIXED IN WITH THE CANDY COATING. The cake balls may not be firm enough. Chill them a little longer before dipping. If you use dark-colored cake, such as chocolate or red velvet, with lighter-colored candy coatings, some crumbs may show up anyway. If so, just redip them in a new batch of melted candy coating.

YOU CAN SEE YOUR CAKE THROUGH THE CANDY COATING. When you use dark-colored cake and white or light-colored candy coatings, this can happen. To make the coating completely opaque, dip the cake balls a second time.

YOUR CANDY COATING HAS A GRAYISH, FILMY-LOOKING SURFACE. "Bloom" can be caused by improper storage of candy coating or changes in temperature when shipping. To avoid this, properly store your coatings in a cool, dry place away from direct heat or sunlight, and avoid temperature changes. When purchasing candy coating from a store, pick out the package with the least amount of bloom, to get off to a good start. FYI: Coatings affected by bloom may not be as pretty, but they are still safe to eat.

Cake Pops Projects

This section features ten ideas for decorating cake pops. From simple projects like the Spring Chicks to those that require a bit more attention to detail like the Burger Bites, you'll be amazed at how easily sprinkles and candy pieces can transform average shapes into fabulous cake creations. The cake pops included here will get you started, and you'll be inspired to unleash your creativity and make something unique. Believe me, once you start making these, it's hard to stop.

Whether you use a mix, bake from scratch, or purchase a store-bought cake to play with, these ideas are about having sweet fun. So grab some cake and frosting, get out some candy coating and lollipop sticks, and let's get started.

Penguins

Your little dippers will love these cake pops and their little flippers.

TO DECORATE

1. Have the oval cake balls chilled and in the refrigerator.

2. Melt the white candy coating in a microwave-safe plastic bowl, following the instructions on the package. The coating should be about 3 in/7.5 cm deep for easier dipping. (I usually work with about 1 lb/455 g of coating at a time.)

3. Tint the coating with black candy coloring. Keep adding color, stirring until the coating is dark enough.

4. When you are ready to dip, remove a few cake balls from the refrigerator at a time, keeping the rest chilled.

5. One at a time, dip about ½ in/12 mm of the tip of a lollipop stick into the melted candy coating, and insert the stick straight into the bottom of a shaped cake ball, pushing it no more than halfway through. Dip the cake pop into the melted coating, and tap off any excess coating, as described in step 12 of Basic Cake Pops, page 24.

6. Before the coating sets, attach a black-coated sunflower seed on either side of the cake pop and place in the stand to dry. (Decorate 12 cake pops at a time if using the stand or use an additional Styrofoam block to accommodate all 48 cake pops.)

continued

YOU'LL NEED

48 uncoated Basic Cake Balls (page 17), formed into oval shapes

3 lb/1.4 kg white candy coating, plus 12 oz/340 g

Deep, microwave-safe plastic bowl

Black candy coloring (not food coloring)

48 paper lollipop sticks

96 black-coated sunflower seeds

Cake Pop Stand or a Styrofoam block

Squeeze bottle

Toothpicks

48 orange rainbow chip sprinkles

96 orange flower sprinkles

Black edible-ink pen

Red Rips Licorice Belts (optional)

Red M&M's (optional)

7. Melt the 12 oz/340 g white candy coating and pour into a squeeze bottle. Pipe the white part of the penguin's body on front of the pop. The shape should look like a heart without any sharp points. Pipe carefully so the white coating doesn't drip around the pop.

8. Let dry completely in the stand.

9. When dry, use a toothpick to dot a small amount of white melted candy coating in position for the beak, and attach an orange rainbow chip sprinkle. Use the same technique using black coating to attach two orange flower sprinkles at the bottom for feet.

10. Draw eyes with a black edible-ink pen, and let dry completely in the stand.

11. If you like, add earmuffs. Cut up strips of Rips Licorice Belt candies and attach across some of the penguin's heads with a bit of melted coating. Then just attach an M&M (M-side down) on either side.

12. Store them in an airtight container on the counter or in the refrigerator for several days. If you are giving them away as gifts, you can cover and tie them with the treat bags and ribbon and add gift tags.

Owls

**These cake pops are a hoot with their
big eyes and sprinkle feet.**

TO DECORATE

1. Have the rounded triangular cake balls chilled and in the refrigerator.

2. Melt the chocolate candy coating in a microwave-safe plastic bowl, following the instructions on the package. The coating should be about 3 in/7.5 cm deep for easier dipping. (I usually work with about 1 lb/455 g at a time.)

3. When you are ready to dip, remove a few cake balls from the refrigerator at a time, keeping the rest chilled.

4. One at a time, dip about ½ in/12 mm of the tip of a lollipop stick into the melted candy coating, and insert the stick straight into the pointed tip of the triangular cake ball, pushing it no more than halfway through. Dip the bottoms of two chocolate chips into the melted candy coating, and attach them to the top of the head for "ears." Hold them in place until the candy coating sets like glue, and place in the stand. (Decorate 12 cake pops at a time if using the stand or use an additional Styrofoam block to accommodate all 48 cake pops.)

5. Dip the cake pops into the melted candy coating, one at a time, as described in step 12 of Basic Cake Pops, page 24. Make sure the coating is deep enough so you can get the entire cake pop, with ears attached, submerged in one dunk. Remove and gently tap off any excess coating.

continued

YOU'LL NEED

48 uncoated Basic Cake Balls (page 17), formed into rounded triangular shapes

3 lb/1.4 kg chocolate candy coating

Deep, microwave-safe plastic bowl

48 paper lollipop sticks

96 chocolate chips

Cake Pop Stand or Styrofoam block

Toothpicks

96 white candy necklace pieces

48 orange rainbow chip sprinkles

96 small pink flower sprinkles

96 brown M&M's Minis

6. Place in the stand to dry.

7. When dry, use a toothpick to dot a small amount of melted candy coating in position for the eyes and attach two white candy necklace pieces.

8. Using the same technique, dot candy coating in position for the beak, and attach an orange rainbow chip sprinkle. Then attach two pink flower sprinkles for the feet and two brown M&M's Minis for the wings.

9. Let dry completely in the stand.

10. Store them in an airtight container on the counter or in the refrigerator for several days. If you are giving them away as gifts, you can cover and tie them with the treat bags and ribbon and add gift tags.

Spring Chicks

**These adorable spring chicks are just the treat to add
some pop to your Easter celebration.**

TO DECORATE

1. Have the cake balls chilled and in the refrigerator.

2. Melt the yellow candy coating in a microwave-safe plastic bowl, following the instructions on the package. The coating should be about 3 in/7.5 cm deep for easier dipping. (I usually work with about 1 lb/455 g of coating at a time.)

3. When you are ready to dip, remove a few cake balls from the refrigerator at a time, keeping the rest chilled.

4. One at a time, dip about ½ in/12 mm of the tip of a lollipop stick into the melted candy coating, and insert the stick straight into a cake ball, pushing it no more than halfway through. Dip the cake pop into the melted coating, and tap off any excess coating, as described in step 12 of Basic Cake Pops, page 24.

5. Let dry completely in the stand. (Decorate 12 cake pops at a time if using the stand or use an additional Styrofoam block to accommodate all 48 cake pops.)

6. When dry, use a toothpick to dot a small amount of melted candy coating in position for the beak, and attach an orange rainbow chip sprinkle. Use the same technique to attach two yellow rainbow chips for wings on either side of the cake pop and two orange flower sprinkles at the bottom for feet.

continued

YOU'LL NEED

48 uncoated Basic Cake Balls (page 17)

3 lb/1.4 kg yellow candy coating

Deep, microwave-safe plastic bowl

48 paper lollipop sticks

Cake Pop Stand or a Styrofoam block

Toothpicks

48 orange rainbow chip sprinkles

96 yellow rainbow chip sprinkles

96 orange flower sprinkles

Black edible-ink pen

7. Draw eyes with a black edible-ink pen, and let dry completely in the stand.

8. Store them in an airtight container on the counter or in the refrigerator for several days. If you are giving them away as gifts, you can cover and tie them with the treat bags and ribbon and add gift tags.

Tip

- Try ditching the sticks. They're pretty cute without them. Just form a cake ball into a pear shape and drop it into a bowl of melted candy coating. Cover it with the coating without moving or stirring it around in the bowl. Then lift it from the coating with a spoon. Tap off the excess coating and slide the little chick carefully off your spoon onto wax paper to set. If the coating pools at the bottom, use a toothpick to draw a separation line. That way, once it dries completely, it will be easier to break off the part you don't want.

Panda Bears

These little bears are black and white and cute all over.

TO DECORATE

1. Have the cake balls chilled and in the refrigerator.

2. Prepare the panda ears. Cut off one-third of each M&M with a sharp knife and use the remaining two-thirds for the ears. Set aside.

3. Melt the white candy coating in a microwave-safe plastic bowl, following the instructions on the package. The coating should be about 3 in/7.5 cm deep for easier dipping. (I usually work with about 1 lb/455 g of coating at a time.)

4. When you are ready to dip, remove a few cake balls from the refrigerator at a time, keeping the rest chilled.

5. One at a time, dip about ½ in/12 mm of the tip of a lollipop stick into the melted candy coating, and insert the stick straight into a cake ball, pushing it no more than halfway through. Dip the cake pop into the melted coating, and tap off any excess coating, as described in step 12 of Basic Cake Pops, page 24.

6. While the coating is still wet, attach two of the M&M's pieces in position for the ears. Hold in place for a few seconds until the candy coating sets like glue, and place in the stand to dry. (Decorate 12 cake pops at a time if using the stand or use an additional Styrofoam block to accommodate all 48 cake pops.)

continued

YOU'LL NEED

48 uncoated Basic Cake Balls (page 17)

96 black M&M's

Small, sharp knife

3 lb/1.4 kg white candy coating

Deep, microwave-safe plastic bowl

48 paper lollipop sticks

Cake Pop Stand or Styrofoam block

Toothpicks

48 miniature black heart sprinkles

Black candy writer

96 miniature white confetti sprinkles

Black edible-ink pen

Pink heart sprinkles, blue heart sprinkles, and blue confetti sprinkles (optional; see Tip)

7. When dry, use a toothpick to dot a small amount of melted candy coating in position for the nose, and attach one miniature black heart sprinkle.

8. Use a black candy writer to pipe a little coating on either side of the nose, in position for the eyes. Attach two miniature white confetti sprinkles before the coating sets. Let dry completely.

9. Use the black edible-ink pen to draw on the mouth and pupils for the eyes.

10. Place in the stand to dry.

11. Store them in an airtight container on the counter or in the refrigerator for several days. If you are giving them away as gifts, you can cover and tie them with the treat bags and ribbon and add gift tags.

Tip

- To make girl pandas, use a pink heart sprinkle for the nose. You can also make a bow using two blue heart sprinkles, attached with the pointed ends facing each other, and one blue confetti sprinkle overlapping the center. Attach each piece by using a toothpick to apply melted candy coating as glue.

Buzzing Bumblebees

**Candy coating wafers can be used for dipping and for decorating.
Here they're used for bumblebee wings.**

TO DECORATE

1. Have the oval-shaped cake balls chilled and in the refrigerator.

2. Melt the yellow candy coating in a microwave-safe plastic bowl, following the instructions on the package. The coating should be about 3 in/7.5 cm deep for easier dipping. (I usually work with about 1 lb/455 g of coating at a time.)

3. When you are ready to dip, remove a few cake balls from the refrigerator at a time, keeping the rest chilled.

4. One at a time, dip about ½ in/12 mm of the tip of a lollipop stick into the melted candy coating, and insert the stick straight into the side of an oval-shaped cake ball, pushing it no more than halfway through. Dip the cake pop into the melted coating, and tap off any excess coating, as described in step 12 of Basic Cake Pops, page 24.

5. For antennae, insert two chocolate jimmies into each bumblebee cake pop while the coating is still wet. Place in the stand to dry. Repeat until all the cake pops have antennae. (Decorate 12 cake pops at a time if using the stand or use an additional Styrofoam block to accommodate all 48 cake pops.)

continued

YOU'LL NEED

48 uncoated Basic Cake Balls (page 17), formed into oval shapes

3 lb/1.4 kg yellow candy coating

Deep, microwave-safe plastic bowl

48 paper lollipop sticks

96 chocolate jimmies

Cake Pop Stand or a Styrofoam block

Large, round cookie cutter

96 white candy coating wafers

Black candy writer

Toothpicks

Black edible-ink pen

6. Prepare the wings. Use the edge of a large, round cookie cutter to cut away a curved shape from each white candy coating wafer. The curved cut should be similar in shape to the side of the cake pop, so you can attach the two without a gap.

7. Use a black candy writer to pipe bumblebee stripes onto the body.

8. Before the black coating dries completely, use a toothpick to apply a small amount of melted yellow coating to the cut side of two of the wing shapes, and attach them to the body. Hold them in place for a few seconds until the candy coating sets like glue, and place in the stand to dry.

9. Use the black edible-ink pen to draw the eyes and mouths, and let dry completely.

10. Store them in an airtight container on the counter or in the refrigerator for several days. If you are giving them away as gifts, you can cover and tie them with the treat bags and ribbon and add gift tags.

Tips

- The antennae and wings may break if they knock against each other, so be careful when moving these.

- Instead of white coating wafers, you can attach 2 white jumbo heart sprinkles to the bumblebees' backs, for a completely different look.

Clowning Around

**Get creative with candy and decorate funny faces
in an assortment of expressions.**

TO DECORATE

1. Have the cake balls chilled and in the refrigerator.

2. Prepare the clown hats first. Using a serrated knife, cut about 1 in/2.5 cm off the tips of several sugar cones and set the tips aside. You won't need the tops of the cones. You don't have to do enough for all the cake pops. Some clowns can be hatless.

3. Melt the white candy coating in a microwave-safe plastic bowl, following the instructions on the package. The coating should be about 3 in/7.5 cm deep for easier dipping. (I usually work with about 1 lb/455 g of coating at a time.)

4. When you are ready to dip, remove a few cake balls from the refrigerator at a time, keeping the rest chilled.

5. One at a time, dip about ½ in/12 mm of the tip of a lollipop stick into the melted candy coating, and insert the stick straight into a cake ball, pushing it no more than halfway through. Dip the cake pop into the melted coating, and tap off any excess coating, as described in step 12 of Basic Cake Pops, page 24.

6. Right after dipping each pop, attach two of the burnt peanut candies in position for the hair, and attach the sugar cone piece on top for the hat. Hold each in place for a few seconds until the candy coating sets like glue. Place the pop in the stand to dry. Repeat until you've used

continued

YOU'LL NEED

48 uncoated Basic Cake Balls (page 17)

Serrated knife

48 or fewer sugar cones

3 lb/1.4 kg white candy coating

Deep, microwave-safe plastic bowl

48 paper lollipop sticks

96 French burnt peanut candies

Cake Pop Stand or a Styrofoam block

Toothpicks

48 red regular or peanut M&M's

Confetti colorstick sprinkles

Life Savers Gummies candies

Fruit Roll-Ups

Rainbow chip sprinkles

Black edible-ink pen

up the sugar cone "hats" and all of the clowns have hair. (Decorate 12 cake pops at a time if using the stand or use an additional Styrofoam block to accommodate all 48 cake pops.)

7. For the face, use a toothpick to dot a small amount of melted candy coating in position for the nose and attach a red M&M (M-side down). Hold it in place until set.

8. Using the same technique, attach two colorstick sprinkles for the eyebrows, using matching colors. Then attach one Life Saver Gummies candy for the collar by sliding it up the lollipop stick and attaching it to the clown head with more melted candy coating. Try cutting out small sections from the candy for a more decorative effect before you attach it.

9. For the mouth, cut a 1-in/2.5-cm rectangular piece of a Fruit Roll-Up and roll it up tightly. Attach it in place, using more melted candy coating as glue.

10. Attach a colored rainbow chip sprinkle on the top of the sugar cone hat with candy coating.

11. Draw eyes with an edible-ink pen and let dry completely in the stand.

12. Store them in an airtight container on the counter or in the refrigerator for several days. If you are giving them away as gifts, you can cover and tie them with the treat bags and ribbon and add gift tags.

Ice Cream Cone Sundaes

**These miniature ice cream cone cake pops
will make a big impression.**

TO DECORATE

1. Have the cake balls chilled and in the refrigerator.

2. Prepare the cones first. Using a serrated knife, cut off the bottoms of the sugar cones so that the width of the opening is about 1¼ in/3 cm inches. You won't need the tops of the cones.

3. Prepare your Styrofoam block. Since these have cone-shaped bottoms, you'll need to do more than just poke holes in the Styrofoam to support them. Take a lollipop stick, insert it into the Styrofoam, and then work it around in a circular motion until you have an opening in the Styrofoam that mimics the bottom shape of the cones.

4. Melt the pink candy coating in a microwave-safe plastic bowl, following the instructions on the package. The coating should be about 3 in/7.5 cm deep. (I usually work with about 1 lb/455 g of coating at a time.)

5. When you are ready to coat, remove a few cake balls from the refrigerator at a time, keeping the rest chilled.

6. Working with one cake ball at a time and using the method for coating as described in step 10 of Basic Cake Balls, page 18, cover a cake ball with the melted coating. Then insert a lollipop stick into the ball to lift it out. Don't worry about any excess coating. Transfer the coated cake ball

continued

YOU'LL NEED

48 uncoated Basic Cake Balls (page 17)

Serrated knife

48 sugar cones

Styrofoam block (Cake Pop Stand not recommended, see Tip on page 58)

Several lollipop sticks

3 lb/1.4 kg pink candy coating

Two deep, microwave-safe plastic bowls

Multicolor sprinkles

1 lb/455 g dark chocolate candy coating

Spoon

48 red peanut M&M's

to the prepared ice cream cone, and remove the stick. Don't worry about the hole left by the stick.

7. The coated cake ball should rest nicely in the opening, and any excess coating will only enhance the look as it drips slightly down the edge. If the cake balls don't fit just right, make another cut in the cones so the opening is smaller, or make the cake balls bigger. Decorate with sprinkles while the pink candy coating is still wet.

8. Place the pops in the Styrofoam block to dry completely.

9. Melt the dark chocolate candy coating. Spoon just a small amount over the very top of the ice cream cone. One at a time, attach a red peanut M&M (M-side down) on top before the chocolate coating sets, and return to the Styrofoam block to dry.

10. Store them in an airtight container on the counter or in the refrigerator for several days. If you are giving them away as gifts, you can cover and tie them with the treat bags and ribbon and add gift tags.

Tips

- I recommend using a Styrofoam block to hold these pops because the diameter of the sugar cone bases makes them less stable in the Cake Pop Stand.

- For a variation, place a coated cake ball on wax paper, add sprinkles, and place the cone at an angle on top of the cake ball; it will look like a fun mistake.

Burger Bites

Dinner and dessert all in one tiny bite. These cake balls, disguised as miniature hamburgers, will trick your senses.

TO DECORATE

1. Have the cake balls chilled and in the refrigerator.

2. Melt the dark chocolate coating in a microwave-safe plastic bowl, following the instructions on the package. The coating should be about 3 in/7.5 cm deep for easier dipping. (I usually work with about 1 lb/455 g of coating at a time.)

3. When you are ready to coat, remove a few cake balls from the refrigerator at a time, keeping the rest chilled.

4. Working with one cake ball at a time and using the method for coating as described in steps 10 and 11 of Basic Cake Balls, page 18, cover a cake ball with the melted coating. Transfer to a wax paper–covered baking sheet to dry. Repeat with the remaining cake balls.

5. If the coating starts to pool around the base of the cake ball, use a toothpick to draw a line through the coating close to the base of the ball. When the coating dries, you can break off any unwanted coating.

6. Melt the red candy coating in a microwave-safe bowl and, holding a cake ball by the top, dip the bottom into the coating, covering it about one-third of the way up. Remove and let the excess coating fall off. Place the ball, red-side

continued

YOU'LL NEED

48 uncoated Basic Cake Balls (page 17)

3 lb/1.4 kg dark chocolate candy coating

Four deep, microwave-safe plastic bowls

Spoons

Wax paper

Baking sheet

Toothpicks

1 lb/455 g red candy coating

1 lb/455 g dark green candy coating

1 lb/455 g peanut butter candy coating

White nonpareils

down, on wax paper and let dry. Repeat with the remaining cake balls. Use the same toothpick trick if pooling happens here.

7. Melt the dark green candy coating in a microwave-safe bowl and, holding a cake ball by the bottom, dip the top into it, coating it about one-third of the way up. Use a toothpick to texturize the coating around the edges for a lettuce leaf-like appearance. Place back on the wax paper, red-side down, and let dry. Repeat with the remaining cake balls.

8. Melt the peanut butter candy coating in a microwave-safe bowl. Again, holding a cake ball by the top, dip the bottom in the coating, leaving some of the red exposed. Return to the wax paper, bottom-side down, to dry completely. Repeat with the remaining cake balls.

9. Once again, dip the top of a cake ball in the peanut butter coating, leaving some of the green "lettuce" visible. Immediately sprinkle white nonpareils on the tops while the coating is wet, and place back on wax paper to dry completely. Repeat with the remaining cake balls.

10. Store them in an airtight container on the counter or in the refrigerator for several days. If you are giving them away as gifts, you can cover and tie them with the treat bags and ribbon and add gift tags.

Tip

- These cake balls are dipped in three layers of candy coating. You can use shortening or paramount crystals to thin the coating so that each layer will not be so thick.

Wedding Cake Pops

These miniature cakes offer mass appeal at parties and receptions.

MAKES 24 TO 36 WEDDING CAKES DEPENDING ON SIZE OF LAYERS

TO DECORATE

1. Have the cake balls chilled and in the refrigerator.

2. Remove the cake balls from the refrigerator and press one ball into each cutter until the mixture fills up the cookie cutter shape. Remove any excess (you can reuse).

3. Remove the shaped mixture from the cookie cutters carefully so the shape stays intact and place on a wax paper–covered baking sheet.

4. Melt the white candy coating in a microwave-safe plastic bowl, following the instructions on the package. The coating should be about 3 in/7.5 cm deep for easier dipping. (I usually work with about 1 lb/455 g of coating at a time.)

5. Apply a thin layer of coating to the bottom of the smaller shaped cake, leaving the center uncoated. (This will make it easier for the lollipop stick to be inserted.)

6. Then place the smaller shaped cake on top of the larger shaped cake, coating-side down. Press gently and let the candy coating set like glue. Place cakes in the refrigerator to keep chilled before dipping.

continued

YOU'LL NEED

48 uncoated Basic Cake Balls (page 17)

One round or crinkle cutter (1½ in/4 cm wide)

One round or crinkle cutter (1¼ in/3 cm wide)

Wax paper

Baking sheet

3 lb/1.4 kg white candy coating

Deep, microwave-safe plastic bowl

48 paper lollipop sticks

48 jumbo pink heart sprinkles

Cake Pop Stand or a Styrofoam block

Squeeze bottle

White sanding sugar

Toothpicks

White confetti sprinkles

7. When you are ready to dip, remove a few stacked cake balls from the refrigerator at a time, keeping the rest chilled.

8. One at a time, dip about ½ in/12 mm of the tip of a lollipop stick into the melted candy coating, and insert the stick straight into the bottom of a stacked cake ball, pushing it no more than halfway through. Dip the cake pop into the melted coating, and tap off any excess coating, as described in step 12 of Basic Cake Pops, page 24.

9. Gently place a jumbo heart sprinkle on top before the coating sets and place in the stand and let dry completely. (Decorate 12 cake pops at a time if using the stand or use an additional Styrofoam block to accommodate all 24 cake pops.)

10. When dry, use a squeeze bottle to pipe more white candy coating on the perimeter of each layer and then sprinkle white sanding sugar on top. You can also use leftover candy coating and a toothpick to glue on white confetti sprinkles. Or get creative and use these as a blank canvas to decorate any way you like.

11. Store them in an airtight container on the counter or in the refrigerator for several days. If you are giving them away as gifts, you can cover and tie them with the treat bags and ribbon and add gift tags.

Rubber Duckies

These little duckies are perfect for a baby shower.

TO DECORATE

1. Have the cake balls chilled and in the refrigerator.

2. Remove the cake balls from the refrigerator and pinch off about one-third of each cake ball and shape it into a tear drop shape and reshape the remaining piece back into a ball. After reshaping, have the cake ball shapes chilled and in the refrigerator.

3. Melt the yellow candy coating in a microwave-safe plastic bowl, following the instructions on the package. The coating should be about 3 in/7.5 cm deep for easier dipping. (I usually work with about 1 lb/455 g of coating at a time.)

4. When you are ready to dip, remove a few cake balls from the refrigerator at a time, keeping the rest chilled. You will stack the two pieces together before dipping. The teardrop shape goes on the bottom of the cake ball.

5. One at a time, dip about ½ in/12 mm of the tip of a lollipop stick into the melted candy coating, and insert the stick straight into both cake balls, pushing it no more than halfway through the second ball. Dip the cake pop into the melted coating, and tap off any excess coating, as described in step 12 of Basic Cake Pops, page 24.

continued

YOU'LL NEED

48 uncoated Basic Cake Balls (page 17)

3 lb/1.4 kg yellow candy coating

Two deep, microwave-safe plastic bowls

48 paper lollipop sticks

96 jumbo orange confetti sprinkles

Cake Pops Stand or a Styrofoam block

Toothpicks

96 candy eyes (see Tip)

12 oz/340 g white candy coating

Small bowl

Sugar pearls

6. Before the coating sets, insert two jumbo orange confetti sprinkles, slightly open, to form the duck's bill. Let dry completely in the stand. (Decorate 12 cake pops at a time if using the stand or use an additional Styrofoam block to accommodate all 48 cake pops.)

7. When dry, use a toothpick to dot a small amount of melted candy coating in position and attach two candy eyes.

8. To give the duckies a bubble bath, melt the white candy coating in a microwave-safe plastic bowl and set aside a small bowl of sugar pearls. Carefully remove the lollipop stick by slowly twisting it out from the pop. Dip the duck's bottom into the white candy coating and then into the sugar pearls. Reinsert the lollipop stick and let dry in the stand.

9. Store them in an airtight container on the counter or in the refrigerator for several days. If you are giving them away as gifts, you can cover and tie them with the treat bags and ribbon and add gift tags.

Tips

- Candy eyes can be found at cake supply stores and even at craft stores. But, you can also pipe eyes on with white candy coating, attach them with sprinkles, or draw them on with a black edible-ink pen.

- Make the duckies without the sugar pearl "bubbles" and they will be ready for springtime.

Displaying, Storing, Shipping & Supplies

So, now you know how to make cake pops. But you may be wondering, "How am I going to present them?" In addition to the treat bags, ribbon, and gift tags in the kit, there are lots of different ways to pretty up a cake pop. Here are several approaches to try. From do-it-yourself displays to professionally built stands, it's easy to make your cake pop creations shine like pop stars.

DISPLAYING YOUR CAKE POPS

THE CAKE POP STAND The 12-pop stand that comes in this kit can be used both for letting the pops dry and presenting them when they are finished. Be sure that the cake pop stick goes through both pieces of cardboard for maximum stability in the stand.

STYROFOAM BLOCKS Also used as a place to allow your cake pops to dry, Styrofoam blocks can be covered in scrapbook paper for a pretty, easy, and inexpensive display, too. Styrofoam is a better choice than the included Cape Pop Stand for pops like the Ice Cream Cone Sundaes because it can be customized to accommodate the unusually sized base of the pop. You can make the block any size you like depending on how many pops you want to display.

Measure your Styrofoam and cut a piece of paper to match the length and width of the block. Use plain paper for this, not decorative paper; it will serve as a template. Using a pencil, make marks on the paper where the holes will be, placing them 2 in/5 cm apart. Place the paper over the Styrofoam and poke through the paper at the marks with the tip of a pencil. Then mark each spot on the Styrofoam with a marker. Remove the paper and use a paper lollipop stick to poke holes into the Styrofoam. Try to insert

the stick as straight into the Styrofoam as possible, without poking all the way through it. Wrap the Styrofoam block in decorative paper. Place the paper template on top of the wrapped Styrofoam and mark the hole locations with a pencil. This time, make a few tiny holes with the end of a needle, so you'll be able to insert the lollipop stick through without messing up the decorative paper. Be careful when removing cake pops from a Styrofoam block. If all the cake pops are removed from one side, the weight of the pops on the other side can cause the Styrofoam to tip over.

GLASSWARE Glass dishes filled with sugar make an eye-pleasing display for cake pops. The dishes should be deep enough to keep the sticks standing upright. You can also fill glass dishes with gumballs, M&M's, or even marbles for a decorative approach.

BOUQUETS You can use a flowerpot or basket to display cake pops. Place a Styrofoam ball or block inside the basket so that it's secure. Then arrange the cake pops in the Styrofoam. You can disguise the Styrofoam by filling in around the sticks with paper confetti, ribbon, streamers, or some other fun decoration.

PAINTED WOOD DISPLAYS You'll need a drill and a ruler for this one. Mark holes 2 in/5 cm apart on a piece of wood that is about 2 in/5 cm thick. Make a mark on the drill bit about 1 3/4 in/4.5 cm from the tip, so that you don't drill all the way through the wood. Drill holes slightly larger than the diameter of the lollipop sticks you are using. Lighter wood with less grain will look the best.

LOLLIPOP STANDS Super-cute premade displays are a great way to go if you're in a hurry. They're also called lollipop trees or sucker displays. Wilton carries a nice one; or if you're feeling crafty, you can make one (see tutorial at www.marthastewartweddings .com/article/lollipop-stand-how-to).

WRAPPING YOUR CAKE POPS

GIFT TAGS You can make your gift even more special by including a sweet note. We've included gift tags in the kit that you can slide onto the stick of the cake pop— some with preprinted happy sayings and some that you can customize with your own personal message.

Or, make your own. Use a 2 in/5 cm paper punch (easily available in craft stores), and punch shapes out of heavyweight card stock. Then use a standard hole-punch to make two holes on either side of the shape. Add a handwritten note, and slide the tag onto the stick. Or use a computer to type-set the message you want on card stock and use a large paper punch to punch around it. You can also visit www.bakerella.com/tags for more downloadable designs.

TREAT BAGS This kit comes with 48 bags sized perfectly to fit most cake pops. Simply wrap each cake pop individually in a treat bag, and tie it up with some of the decorative ribbon. Additional treat bags are easy to find at cake decorating and craft stores (see Supplies, page 77).

RIBBON Six colors of ribbon are included with this kit and can be mixed and matched as you like to coordinate with almost any event. After you wrap a cake pop in a treat bag, select the color ribbon of your choice, cut a piece to about 12 in/30.5 cm, and tie in a pretty bow. Slide a gift tag onto the stick and your cake pop is ready for giving (and making someone happy).

STORING YOUR CAKE POPS

Cake pops made with a cake mix and ready-made frosting can be stored in an airtight container on the counter. If you wrap them individually in treat bags tied with ribbon, they can stand in the Cake Pop Stand or a Styrofoam block until ready to serve.

Cake pops made with homemade ingre-dients that are perishable, such as cream cheese frosting, should be stored in the refrigerator, either in an airtight container or already wrapped in treat bags.

Cake pops will last for several days and can be made a few days before an event. They can also be stored in the freezer if you need to make them further in advance.

Note: Candy coating manufacturers do not recommend storing in the refrigerator or freezer. But I have had success with storing the finished pops when wrapped in treat bags tied with a ribbon and also placing them in an airtight container.

SHIPPING YOUR CAKE POPS

Cake pops are surprisingly easy to ship. Look for pastry boxes to place them in.

Cover cake pops with treat bags and ribbon, and then lay them in alternating directions in a small pastry or cake box. Use tissue paper to fill in any gaps and to keep the pops from sliding around in the box.

Tape the box shut and place it in a larger box surrounded by packing material. Ship them overnight to ensure freshness.

SUPPLIES

CAKE- AND CANDY-MAKING *Candy coatings, lollipop sticks, treat bags, and more can be found at the following online sources.*

Cake Art:
www.cakeartpartystore.com

Candyland Crafts:
www.candylandcrafts.com

CK Products:
www.ckproducts.com

Confectionery House:
www.confectioneryhouse.com

Kitchenkrafts.com:
www.kitchenkrafts.com

CANDY *Grocery stores, drug stores, and even gas stations carry a wide assortment of candies to get your creative juices flowing. Here are a few online options as well.*

Candy Direct:
www.candydirect.com

Candy Warehouse:
www.candywarehouse.com

Dylan's Candy Bar:
www.dylanscandybar.com

M&M's:
www.mms.com
(purchase the color you want)

CANDY COATINGS *Find chocolate, vanilla, and colored candy coatings from a variety of outlets. Chocolate and vanilla varieties are also available from the Kroger grocery store chain.*

Kroger:
www.kroger.com

Make 'n Mold:
www.makenmold.com

Merckens:
www.adm.com and available from cake and candy suppliers

Wilton:
www.wilton.com

CANDY COLORING

Chefmaster Candy Color:
available from cake and candy suppliers

Make 'n Mold:
www.makenmold.com

Wilton:
www.wilton.com

CANDY OIL

LorAnn Oils:
www.lorannoils.com

EDIBLE-INK PENS

Americolor:
www.americolorcorp.com

FLOWER COOKIE CUTTERS (FOR CUPCAKE POPS)

Ateco (available in mini-cutter set #4848)

Wilton (available in mini sets)

CRAFT STORES *Retail craft stores also carry most of the basics you'll need for many of the projects, including treat bags, ribbon, and lollipop sticks.*

A.C. Moore:
www.acmoore.com

Hobby Lobby:
www.hobbylobby.com

Jo-Ann Fabric and Craft Stores:
www.joann.com

Michaels:
www.michaels.com

Index